Teacher

Teacher

Bonnie Juettner

**RAINTREE
STECK-VAUGHN
PUBLISHERS**

A Harcourt Company

Austin New York
www.steck-vaughn.com

Published by Raintree Steck-Vaughn Publishers,
an imprint of Steck-Vaughn Company

Art Director: Max Brinkmann
Editor: Pam Wells
Design and Illustration: Proof Positive/Farrowlyne Associates, Inc.
Planned and Produced by
Proof Positive/Farrowlyne Associates, Inc.

Library of Congress Cataloging-in-Publication Data
Juettner, Bonnie.
  Teacher/Bonnie Juettner.
    p. cm. — (Workers you know)
  Summary: A teacher describes the many aspects of his job and the training and skills needed in this important profession.
  ISBN 0-8172-5595-8
    1. Teachers—Juvenile literature. 2. Teaching—Vocational guidance—Juvenile literature.
  [1. Teachers. 2. Teaching. 3. Occupations.] I. Title. II. Series.

LB1775 .J74 2000
371.2—dc21

99–055961

Printed and bound in the United States
1 2 3 4 5 6 7 8 9 0 LB 03 02 01 00

Acknowledgments:
Photo Credits: **10–11:** © Wolfgang Kaehler/Corbis

Note: You will find more information about becoming a teacher on the last page of this book.

Do you like to solve problems? Many people have to solve problems every day at work. A mechanic might have to figure out why a car won't run. A doctor has to figure out what's wrong when people get sick or hurt. And me—well, my name is Christopher Lee, and I'm a teacher. I have to figure out ways to help children learn. Let me tell you about a time when I had a big problem to solve.

Teacher

The week before school started, I was in my classroom getting ready for my students. I reviewed what I was going to teach that year. I hung pictures on the bulletin board at the back of the room. I made name tags for each student. As I was checking to make sure I had all my supplies, the principal entered. He told me that none of my textbooks would be at school for the first week.

Principal Rivera

After I finished talking with Principal Rivera, I was worried. I had worked hard on my lesson plan, the outline of what I was going to teach. But the lesson plan depended on my students' having books. What was I going to do? Then I had an idea.

The next morning I introduced myself to the class. I took attendance to make sure everyone was there. All 25 students were in their seats. Next, I asked students to name the biggest plant they could think of.

I was happy to see so many of my students raise their hands to answer. I like to start the school year with a discussion. It gives my students a chance to know me, and it gives me a chance to know them. I try to let them talk about something they already know. Then, I move from the things they know to the things they don't know much about yet—the things I want to teach them.

Sometimes, teachers have to talk for a long time while students listen. But I like it when we figure things out together. My students and I talked about plants for a few minutes. Then, I explained that we were about to start a unit on trees.

I had kept our discussion short on purpose, because I wanted to show my students around the classroom. My classroom is divided into areas where students can work on different projects. The bulletin board is part of my science center. The bulletin board shows a dinosaur, a whale, and a sequoia (si-**kwoy**-a) tree next to each other, because I want students to notice that the sequoia is the biggest. When I use amazing facts like this in my teaching, my students get excited. Then they want to learn more.

The science center is also the area where I keep the science tools we use. Sometimes we need to measure things, so I keep measuring cups and a scale handy. We'll use the blocks and the spools later, when we learn about simple machines.

I told my students, while we were studying trees and plants, that they could plant seeds in this area. Then, the class could watch the seeds as they grew. I usually ask my students to write what they see in their science journals. Looking at the natural world is a great way to learn about science.

Teacher

Of course, science isn't the only subject that I teach. I also teach language arts, social studies, geography, and mathematics. I try to help students connect all these different subjects to each other.

In my social studies corner, I have a map of the world. What does that have to do with the trees we're learning about in science? I've added some special features to the world map. My map has a tree line near each pole. This reminds my students of the areas on Earth where trees can't grow. Between the tree lines, I've added pictures, showing what kinds of trees grow in different parts of the world. Different trees grow in different areas because the climate and the soil are different. For example, the ginkgo (**gin**-ko) tree grows in China!

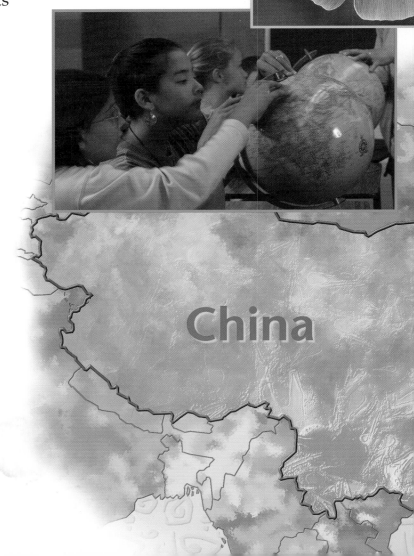

China

Angela Benton

Books, papers, pencils, computers—this part of my room is for reading and writing. Right now, I have lots of books about trees in this area. Students can use the books to do research before they start to write.

The recess bell rang just as I was finishing up. "Time for recess," I said, and my class hurried out to play. Angela Benton, my teacher aide, went with them. Angela's job is to help me do my job! Sometimes Angela helps to answer questions when the class works in small groups. She also helps me grade tests. During recess, Angela makes sure the children play safely on the playground.

I hurried out too, but not to play. I had to get to the library before recess ended. Even when I am not teaching, I am still planning and working.

I had made it through one lesson without textbooks. But it was only Monday. I needed to make lesson plans for the rest of the week. That's why I headed for the library. For teachers, the library is like a big toolbox. It's full of tools that teachers need to help them teach their classes.

Adam Hirsch, the librarian, helps me find just the right materials in the school library, so that I can teach interesting lessons. This time, Adam helped me find books about trees. He also gave me advice about how to find interesting sites about trees on the Internet. Then, Adam told me he would set up a special exhibit about trees, right there in the library! He would put pictures of trees on the library bulletin board. He also planned to show books about trees on the tables and on the shelves.

Adam
Hirsch

After my students came back from recess, it was time for reading. I opened my library books and read several poems about nature to the class.

Teacher

Everyone talked about the meaning of the poems. Then, I asked each student to write a poem about a tree or something in nature.

After they finished, I had a meeting with each student and talked about what each had written. We talked about their use of words and how they felt when they were writing. We talked about ways to make their poems better. I think talking with my students about writing helps them to write better.

I often use special tools in my classroom. Sometimes I show movies and filmstrips. Sometimes I use models, like my model of the planets in our solar system. This way my students can see how something works. For my history lesson, I used my laptop computer and a projector. Because trees grow a new ring of bark around their trunks every year, I used a picture of the rings inside a tree trunk to make a time line. This showed the years of the American Revolutionary War.

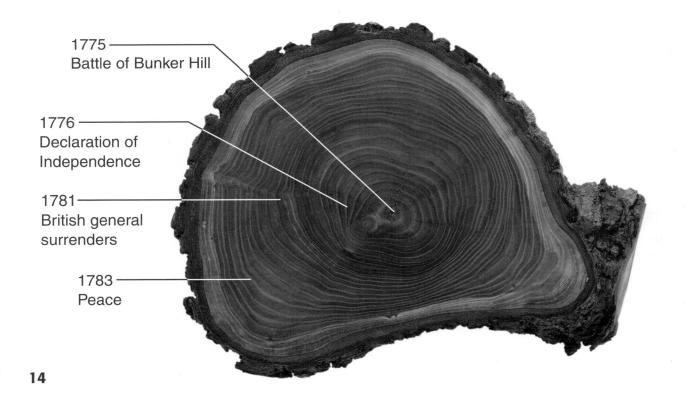

1775
Battle of Bunker Hill

1776
Declaration of
Independence

1781
British general
surrenders

1783
Peace

Using a computer is something I just learned how to do. I learned it in summer school. During the school year and in the summer, I take classes so I can learn new things to share with my students. Teachers expect students to learn, but it's important for us to keep learning new things, too.

When the bell rang at the end of the day, my class said good-bye and went home. But I couldn't go home yet. I had a teachers' meeting to attend. At the meeting, Mr. Rivera told all the teachers about the new career-education curriculum (ker-**ick**-kew-lum) we were going to teach. A curriculum is a subject— like math, science, language arts—and the way it is taught in each grade. He also told us about the plans for parent-teacher conferences, or meetings, to be held the following week. We talked about what we wanted to say to the parents.

Notice how few rings this younger tree has.

The next day, my students got a big surprise. We were going to go on a field trip to the forest preserve, a special park full of plants and animals.

Field trips are another way to get students excited about learning. I especially like the forest preserve, but I have also taken students to museums and factories. Almost anywhere we visit, we can find something new to learn.

Before the students left school for the day, I gave them permission slips. Before I can take students anywhere off the school grounds, I have to make sure everyone has permission from a parent or guardian to go. I also have to arrange for a school bus to take us there.

School District #93
PERMISSION SLIP

_____ permission to
I give my child _____
participate in the field trip to _____
on _____ .

It is agreed that no liability is assumed by the school, school employees or school authorized personnel for injuries to persons or damage to property while on the above field trip.

_____
(signature of parent or guardian)
_____
(date)

My students were very excited on the day of the field trip. I reminded them that learning doesn't only happen in a classroom. For the day, the forest preserve would be our school.

My students stopped in front of almost every tree they found. They wrote in their journals about what they saw. They used measuring tapes to measure the distance around each tree trunk. They used their magnifying glasses to look more closely at different kinds of pine tress. They collected leaves, seeds, and soil. We put everything we collected into plastic bags. We labeled each bag with the name of the tree, the date, and the place we found it. When you work on science projects, it's important to be neat and organized.

Teacher

field trip

17

As we walked through the trees, one of my students found a tree seed. She wanted to know what kind of tree it came from. I told her to look it up in her field guide. A field guide is a special book about nature. It can tell you about animals, plants, rocks, and lots of other things.

I could just tell my students the answers to their questions. But I want my students to learn how to be their own teachers. I teach them to think about what they know, research what they don't know, and figure out the answers to their own questions. That way, they can keep learning even when they have no teachers to teach them.

Teacher

Tom
Shanis

Tom Shanis, our school's music teacher, came with us on the field trip. On the way back to school in the bus, Tom led us in a music lesson. First, we sang songs about trees. Then we made up a song about trees. We used the tune to "Skip to My Lou." We called our song "Plant Me a Tree."

I wrote down the words to the song. I had a feeling we might want to sing this song again sometime.

When we arrived back at school, we unpacked the leaves, seeds, and soil we had collected. Then, I divided the class into small groups. Each group took the soil from one area of the forest preserve.

I gave each group a microscope and a set of slides and coverslips. Next, I passed out some information about different types of soil. The groups took turns looking at the soil under the microscope. The lenses of the microscope make small objects appear larger. Students compared the sizes of the dirt pieces with the sizes of dirt pieces in the chart I gave them. Then, they tried to figure out what type of soil we had brought back from the forest preserve.

My students found some sand and clay in the soil. Sand has big pieces that let water drain through. Clay has tiny pieces that hold too much water for most plants.

The students also found other pieces in the soil. They were very small pieces, but they were big enough to let some water drain out, so the soil didn't hold too much water. Plants need just the right amount of water to grow—not too much or too little.

Teacher

Everyone learns differently. Some people learn best by looking at pictures. Other people learn best by listening to a story. Still other people learn best by making things. All these ways of learning are important. That's why I use different kinds of activities in all of my lessons.

I'm always glad to have people from the town come and talk to my class. These people have a lot of experience because they have been working a long time. They are resources, just like books and videos.

Mr. Marzullo, who works for the forest preserve, offered to talk to the students. Before he came, we made a list of the questions we wanted to ask him. Our trip to the forest preserve and our soil experiment really helped us to ask good questions. And Mr. Marzullo answered every one!

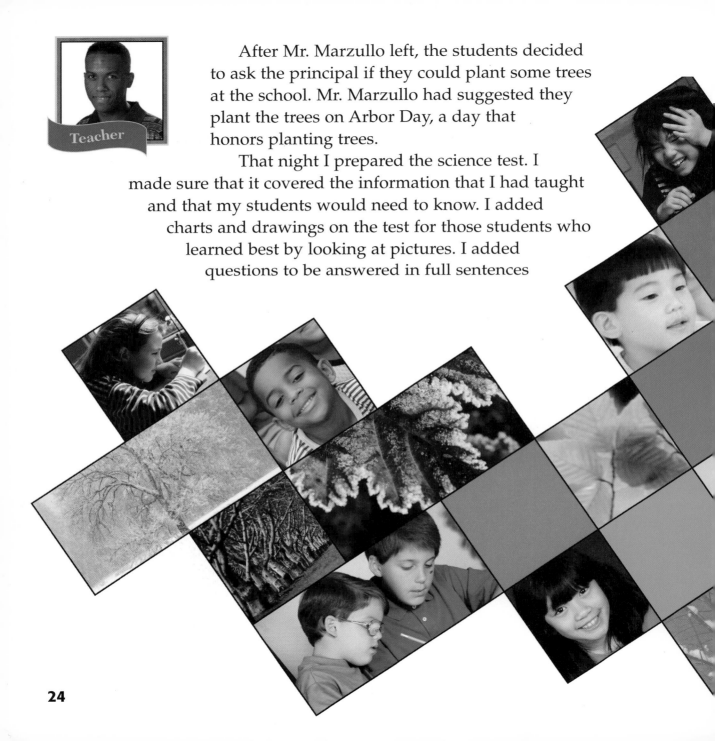

After Mr. Marzullo left, the students decided to ask the principal if they could plant some trees at the school. Mr. Marzullo had suggested they plant the trees on Arbor Day, a day that honors planting trees.

That night I prepared the science test. I made sure that it covered the information that I had taught and that my students would need to know. I added charts and drawings on the test for those students who learned best by looking at pictures. I added questions to be answered in full sentences or in a paragraph, so my students could explain what they learned.

Some of my students get nervous when they have to take a test, and I don't blame them. I know what it's like to take tests, because I had to take a lot of tests when I was in school. And after I finished college, I had to take a state test to receive a license to teach.

Part of my job is to keep careful track of student grades on tests and homework assignments. I also have to keep track of how they perform on class projects. That's because I have to prepare report cards for each student in my class. I use a lot of math when I figure out final grades. I use addition and division.

When I meet with parents, I like to show them the results of the tests their children have taken. We also talk about what my students have liked about the school year.

Sometimes I ask the students to present their work at these meetings. I think they can talk much better about what they've done than I can. It's also important that they hear what their parents and I are saying. They can say things, too. That way, everyone knows what the goals are for the coming months.

Teacher

The next day, we divided into three tree-planting teams—each with a special job. One team had to find out what type of soil we had. Another team had to research our climate and find out what type of trees would grow best. Another team would have to ask the school board to give us permission to plant trees on the school grounds.

While my students were working, Principal Rivera stopped by. Part of his job is to visit classrooms and make sure students are learning. He also makes sure I am teaching according to the plans he has asked us to follow.

We planted our seeds on Wed. April 26th

We have been growing our garden for this many days:

Mr. Rivera wasn't the only one to visit my classroom that day. Some other teachers stopped by while their classes were at recess. They wanted to have their classes help with the tree project. Sometimes it's fun to have our classes work together on one big project.

Mrs. Anderson, the art teacher, had a great idea. She would have the students draw pictures of the way trees grow from seeds. They could trace the drawings onto cloth squares. Then they could sew the squares together to make an Arbor Day quilt.

Mrs. Anderson

28

I'm almost glad that our books didn't come this week. When I was a student, I enjoyed learning by doing so many different things. I decided to become a teacher so that I could help other people learn. So I studied math, science, music, art, and language arts in college. And I took classes in how to teach. I also practiced teaching students. In that class, I was given a grade on my teaching ability by a more experienced teacher. She also told me how I could teach better.

During the year, we worked on the project once a week. On Arbor Day our hard work paid off. We planted six young trees in front of our school. Remember "Plant Me a Tree," the song we made up on the way home from our field trip? We sang it while we planted the new trees. And we hung the Arbor Day quilt in the school lobby for everyone to admire.

When we were finished planting, we celebrated. Everyone from the school and lots of people from our town were part of the celebration. As I watched the students planting trees, I thought

about how much we had all learned during this school year. I remembered how nervous I was at the beginning. I never would have believed that this would turn into my best year of teaching. While I was teaching the students, they were teaching me—giving me new ideas to explore, and, most of all, teaching me how much I love my job.

Teacher

For Information About Becoming a Teacher, Contact:
American Federation of Teachers
555 New Jersey Avenue, NW
Washington, DC 20001

Association for Childhood Education International
11501 Georgia Avenue, Suite 315
Wheaton, MD 20902-1924

Teacher Training, Education, and Requirements:
Most states require teachers to complete four years of approved college work and have a bachelor's degree. Most states require elementary teachers to have their bachelor's degree in elementary education. As part of their undergraduate education, most teachers work as assistant teachers, working in real classrooms alongside experienced teachers. In addition to a degree, most states require that elementary teachers pass a certification test.

Related Careers:
Principal
Librarian
Recreation Leader
Camp Counselor
School Psychologist
Social Worker

4/01

NEW HANOVER COUNTY PUBLIC LIBRARY
201 Chestnut Street
Wilmington, N.C. 28401

GAYLORD R